Johann Paul von Westhoff

Six Suites for Solo Violin

transcribed and edited by

Dr. Sarah Jones-Hayes

WWW. MELBAY.COM

Contents

Introduction

Johann Paul von Westhoff, (born in Dresden 1656, buried in Weimar in 1705), was among the top violinist/composers of his time along with Heinrich Ignaz Franz Biber and Johann Jakob Walther. His works for violin, both solo and accompanied, hold enormous historical and musical significance. They contributed to the development and establishment of the violin as a virtuosic instrument and inspired the continued development and direction of polyphonic writing for solo violin.

Unknown until their discovery was announced in 1971 by Péter Várnai in an article in *Die Musikforschung*, this set of six suites for solo violin, published in 1696, is in all likelihood a second edition of or second collection to his *First Dozen Allemandes, Courantes, Sarabands and Gigues for Solo Violin without Basso Continuo* published in 1682 which are considered lost. Along with his suite for solo violin published in 1683 in *Le Mercure Galant,* these suites for unaccompanied violin are the first in their medium. Westhoff also composed a sonata for violin and basso continuo, published in *Le Mercure Galant* in 1682 and a set of six sonatas for violin and basso continuo, published in Dresden in 1694.

The set of six suites, published in 1696 and presented in this publication, was discovered in the Somogyi Károly Városi és Megyei Könyvtár in Szeged, Hungary and is the only original 1696 publication known to exist. Because the title page is missing, the title of the collection is unknown. The last page, containing the B section of the gigue in Suite No.VI, is also missing so I have added my own B section as a substitute. I obtained a facsimile of the original 1696 publication on my visit to Szeged and have included it in the back of this edition as a reference.

Not only were these suites the first in their genre, they were also important precursors to what is arguably the most important set of solo works in the violin repertoire and one of the most monumental compositions in all of Western history- Johann Sebastian Bach's *Six Sonatas and Partitas for Unaccompanied Violin.* In 1703, Johann Sebastian Bach came to work in Weimar where Westhoff was also employed. Without a doubt, Westhoff's compositions inspired Bach to compose his own set of sonatas and partitas which he composed between 1703 and 1720.

Aside from their historical significance, Westhoff's collection of suites provide an excellent tool for preparing students to study solo Bach. In my opinion, there is very little in terms of standard repertoire that adequately prepares students for the study of solo Bach. While these suites provide many challenges, they are shorter and musically simpler than Bach's Sonatas and Partitas, which make them much more accessible.

Westhoff's notation is unique, featuring a stave with eight lines and two clefs. While transcribing these into modern notation, I changed the time signature of several movements for ease of reading and corrected the key signatures of Suites II and V. All fingerings, dashed slurs, and parenthetical accidentals are editorial and serve only as suggestions. Ultimately, it is up to the performer to create their own convincing interpretation. It is important for students to understand that music composed during Westhoff's time was written with the understanding that the given notes provided a framework from which the performer would interpret, ornament, and improvise. Composers did not dictate every dynamic, nuance, or embellishment. Instead, they left the responsibility of interpretation to the performer. Below, are a few musical and technical challenges students will need to take into consideration along with an explanation of a few editorial decisions.

The *signum congruentiae,* or sign of congruence (·𝄋·) is a term that has been used to describe a symbol which has taken on a variety of shapes and meanings in sources as far back as the 1400s. The theorist, Anonymous 12, describes its function in polyphonic music as the point where all voices come together. It has been described by other theorists as the point in a canonic work where a voice enters. It has also been used to indicate a repeat and ornamentation among other things. Concerning Westhoff's suites, I believe these signs were most likely intended to invite ornamentation and possibly a repeat of the designated passage. If I were to observe the repeat of the entire A or B section indicated in the score, I would only repeat the marked passage on the second repeat of the A or B section.

When determining appropriate fingering, it is important to take into consideration the benefit a preference for lower positions and open strings has on the tone, resonance, and variety of colors and voices. Consistency of tone within a voice or passage and a clean execution should also be a priority. Often, the fourth finger or a higher position can and should be used to avoid an unnecessary and potentially sloppy string crossing or an unwanted change in color. In general, it is best to avoid crossing strings for only one note. Not only does the string crossing change the color of that note, but it can also add an unwanted emphasis.

In many polyphonic passages it is not always possible to sustain stationary voices their full value without rearticulating them, which is often not necessary and sometimes inappropriate. Frequently, note values indicate part writing rather than the duration they should sound. When deciding when to rearticulate notes which are notated to sustain against a moving line, the priority needs to be given to the thematic material. Clarity of the melodic line and voice leading should be of utmost importance. Good examples of this can be found throughout the courante in Suite No. I.

Suite No. I in A minor, Courante m. 6-10

The chords, which appear on the first and occasionally the third beats of measures, notate sustained voices over and under a continuous line of eighth notes moving in stepwise motion. These chords outline the harmonic progression and complement changes in the melodic line. It is not possible to sustain these stationary voices together with the moving line without rearticulating them and they should not be rearticulated as the thick texture would obscure the melodic line.

Examples of appropriate places to rearticulate sustained notes can be found throughout the sarabandes in Suite No. I and Suite No. VI. In Westhoff's 1696 edition, there are several instances within these two movements where inside voices are notated to sustain for multiple beats while the other two or three voices move in polyphony. Looking at the second measure below, the original notation sustains the middle voice for three beats. In order to play the chord on the second beat, the B natural in the middle voice would need to be rearticulated to avoid jumping over the A string in the middle of the chord.

Suite No. I in A minor, Sarabande with original note values (transposed from $\frac{3}{1}$ to $\frac{3}{4}$)

Edited version

Because the texture is so continuously thick in these two movements, I thought the score would be easier to read if the inner voices which need to be rearticulated for technical reasons and a few upper voices which should be rearticulated for clear voice leading, were written to reflect a rearticulated rhythm. I kept most of the original bass note notation as it appears in the original. Some bass notes, such as the one in the first measure of the example above, may be rearticulated on the following beat (played as one quarter note followed by one half note) or the performer may decide that the rearticulation of the bass voice is unnecessary. On the other hand, the lower two voices on the downbeats of measures four and eight should not be rearticulated when the eighth note in the top voice is played. The eighth note in the top voice of both measures should sound alone. There are only two other movements where I changed the notation to show a rearticulated note. The first is in the courante in Suite No.V, measure twenty. I changed the half-note D-natural on the downbeat into two quarter notes. The second is in the gigue in Suite No. VI, measure ten. I changed the D-natural dotted quarter note on the second beat into a quarter note followed by an eighth note.

When articulating three and four-note chords, there are a variety of factors to take into consideration. In modern practice, it is common (depending on context) to split these chords so that the bottom two notes sound together, slightly before the beat, and the top two voices follow, sounding together on the beat. However, some literature from the 1600's suggests that these chords may have been executed in a manner which more closely resembles an arpeggiation. Multiple sources from the seventeenth century suggest playing the lower pitch first before pulling the bow across the remaining strings to the top pitch. In Thomas Mace's *Musik's Monument,* printed in 1676, he suggests (for final chords) using a good amount of bow on the lowest string and playing it by itself with a swell before sliding the bow across the other strings. Christopher Simpson describes in *The Division-Violist*, printed in 1659, that the lowest string of the viol should sound first and for as long as required before sliding the bow across the other strings to the highest string.

Whether the performer chooses to execute chords in the manner described in the sources above or by breaking most chords two-plus-two, there are many instances where chords must be arpeggiated due to the location of the notes. For example, if two notes in a chord share the same string, they cannot be played simultaneously. There will also be occasions where the performer may decide it is more appropriate or necessary to articulate chords in a manner which comes as close to playing all notes as simultaneously as possible. This would involve playing the chord with as little break or as quick an arpeggiation as possible. An example would be a fast passage featuring continuous three or four-note chords. If each chord is broken two-plus-two or arpeggiated too slowly, not only can it sound cumbersome and repetitive, it can also interfere with the rhythmic integrity of the passage.

Arguments can also be made for occasions where instead of articulating the chord from the bottom to the top voice, the performer might choose to articulate these chords from the top down or even from the bottom to the top followed by a rearticulation of the bass. When deciding how to execute these chords, the performer should take into consideration the direction and origin of the melodic line. In general, if the melodic line initiates from the top of a chord, the top of the chord should be the last note in the chord to sound in order to connect the melodic line from the chord into the subsequent notes. However, in cases where the melodic line departs from or continues through the bass voice, the violinist may choose to articulate the chord starting from the bass, ascend to the top, and finish by rearticulating the bass, all in one bow direction. If the melodic line preceding a chord originates from the highest voice and passes to the bass voice immediately following the chord, the violinist may choose to articulate the chord from the top voice down. If a chord appears in a monophonic passage and the melody line passes through the top note of the chord, it is not necessary for the performer to articulate the chord from the top down and rearticulate the top. Simply articulating the chord from bottom to top is sufficient.

However the performer decides to execute a chord, care should be given not to unintentionally add or remove weight suddenly when crossing strings to avoid an unwanted accent, interruption, or lack of clarity. The student should imagine their arm weight sinking into the upper strings creating a seamless string crossing. Enough bow weight should be given to the bass note that it speaks clearly. Thoughtful bow distribution should allow the chord to be shaped musically, give the bass note clarity, and save enough bow to sustain the top of the chord for as long as necessary. When possible, all left-hand fingers should be placed before the bow begins to articulate the chord.

Careful consideration needs to be given to bow distribution, weight, and speed in both chords and the melodic line. Just as sudden changes in bow speed or weight when crossing strings in a chord can cause unwanted accents or interruptions, the same applies to the melody line. Take for example, dotted rhythms. If a string player uses a significant amount of bow on the longer note, in order to get back to the opposite end of the bow, the shorter note is often yanked. This can be avoided by using a slower bow on the long note and a lighter, faster bow on the shorter note, or by hooking the notes together.

When deciding bowings, consideration needs to be given to beat hierarchy, articulation, voicing, and character. The allemande in Suite No. I features chords on nearly every beat in the opening measures. If the third and fourth beats in the first full measure are played down-bow and then up-bow respectively, the fourth beat will not be in danger of sounding equal to or greater than the preceding beat. The same can be said for the first and second beats in the second full measure. While it may be easier to use a down-bow to articulate the chords on beats one and two, using two up-bows on the following sixteenth notes, it may sound fairly tedious and unimaginative and may not reflect the beat hierarchy as well.

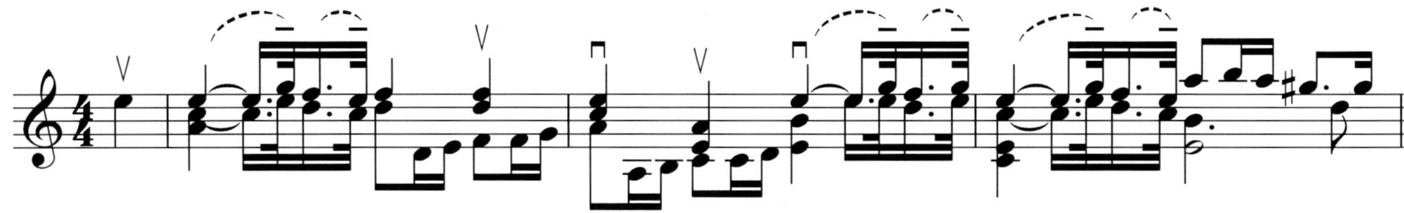

Suite No. I in A minor, Allemande

Another example from the opening of the allemande from Suite No. I is the second beat in the first full measure. This may be played with separate bows in keeping with the original notation, creating a very dance-like character. It may also be played using hooked bows which allow the dotted notes to be more sustained, creating more direction and a longer line.

Unisons using an open string and fourth finger are featured throughout. They are easily executed and make sense musically. However, a few of the more challenging unisons which do not employ an open string beg us to ask whether Westhoff notated these more challenging unisons only to show voice leading. Perhaps too literal a realization of the original notation is not necessary in these cases. An obvious example of a unison that was clearly only written to show voice leading is the first example below from the gigue in Suite No. IV. This unison was either an error, or notated to show good voice leading because it is physically impossible to play the last eighth note on two strings. The other two unisons below are also examples of good part writing and should only be played as one note. I chose not to notate these three unisons in this edition.

Suite No. IV in C Major, Gigue m. 28

Suite No. III in B flat Major, Allemande m. 13

Suite No. VI in D Major, Courante m. 9

If executed well, the following examples make sense musically, show good part writing, and while slightly challenging, are not too difficult to execute. The first example is the last eighth note in measure two of the allemande in Suite No. III which I chose to notate in this edition. I did not notate the unison in the last two examples which I consider optional, so to avoid overwhelming the music with editorial markings. These examples are the last eighth note in measure ten of the gigue in Suite No. II, and the last eighth note in measure two of the gigue in Suite No. III.

All dashed slurs are editorial as are the tenutos which often appear within them. These tenutos were used to indicate separation between notes within the dashed slur, or hooked bowing. While both notes are played in the same bow direction, they should not be legato. They should sound as if they were played using separate bow strokes to imitate their appearance as separate notes in Westhoff's original notation. When these hooked bows appear on dotted figures, the weight should be released from the bow on the dot.

All parenthetical accidentals are suggestions. In modern notation, an accidental is applied to any note which does not belong to the designated key signature. It applies to all notes of that pitch within that octave for the remainder of the measure unless otherwise notated. Before this became a universal practice, music from the 1600s to the late 1700s often show different practices concerning musica ficta, some reflecting older practices and some reflecting newer. This should be taken into consideration when studying Westhoff's notation. Westhoff often applies accidentals to the same pitch every time that pitch repeats within one measure and it is not assumed that an accidental lasts the remainder of a measure within a particular note's octave. Often, a note will appear with a sharp beside it at the beginning of a measure but the same pitch on the last beat, which was not assigned an accidental, will be played as a natural. Westhoff also does not typically notate the accidental on the repetition of a pitch if it is within close proximity to the first pitch.

Phrases should be allowed to breathe, pull back, and push forward as necessary. There are several instances where time needs to be taken at the end of a phrase or a breath needs to be used. Good examples of this are in the sarabande from Suite No. I. The fourth measure going into the fifth measure as well as the transition from the A to the B section, measure twelve into thirteen, and the final cadence, should not sound metronomic or rushed. When taking time, the performer should do so organically.

Suite I

Johann Paul Westhoff

Courante

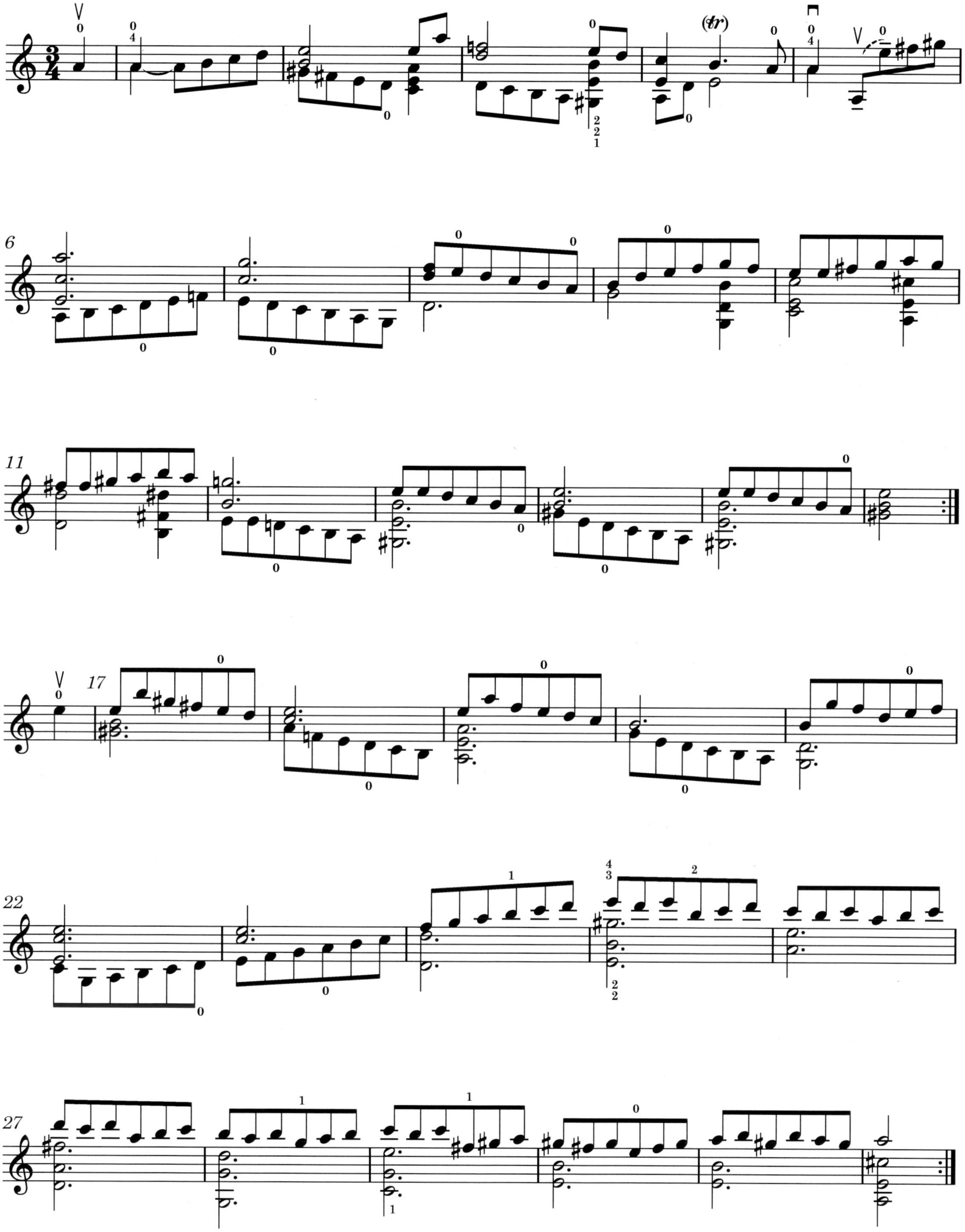

Sarabande

Gigue

Sign of congruence (𝄋): ornament and repeat selected passage.

Suite II

Sarabande

Gigue

Suite III

Allemande

* Suggested execution:

Courante
Sarabande

Gigue

Suite IV

Allemande

Courante

Sarabande

Gigue

7

13

19

p *f*

23

27

32

37

42

Suite V

Allemande

Sign of congruence (·§·): ornament and repeat selected passage.

Courante

Sarabande

Gigue

Suite VI

Allemande

* 1696 edition:

Sign of congruence (·𝄋·): ornament and repeat selected passage.

Sign of congruence (𝄋): ornament and repeat selected passage.

Gigue

The last page, containing the B section of the Gigue, is missing from the only extant 1696 publication. The B section above is a suggested substitute.

Facsimile of the 1696 Publication

courtesy of the Somogyi Károly Városi és Megyei Könyvtár in Szeged, Hungary

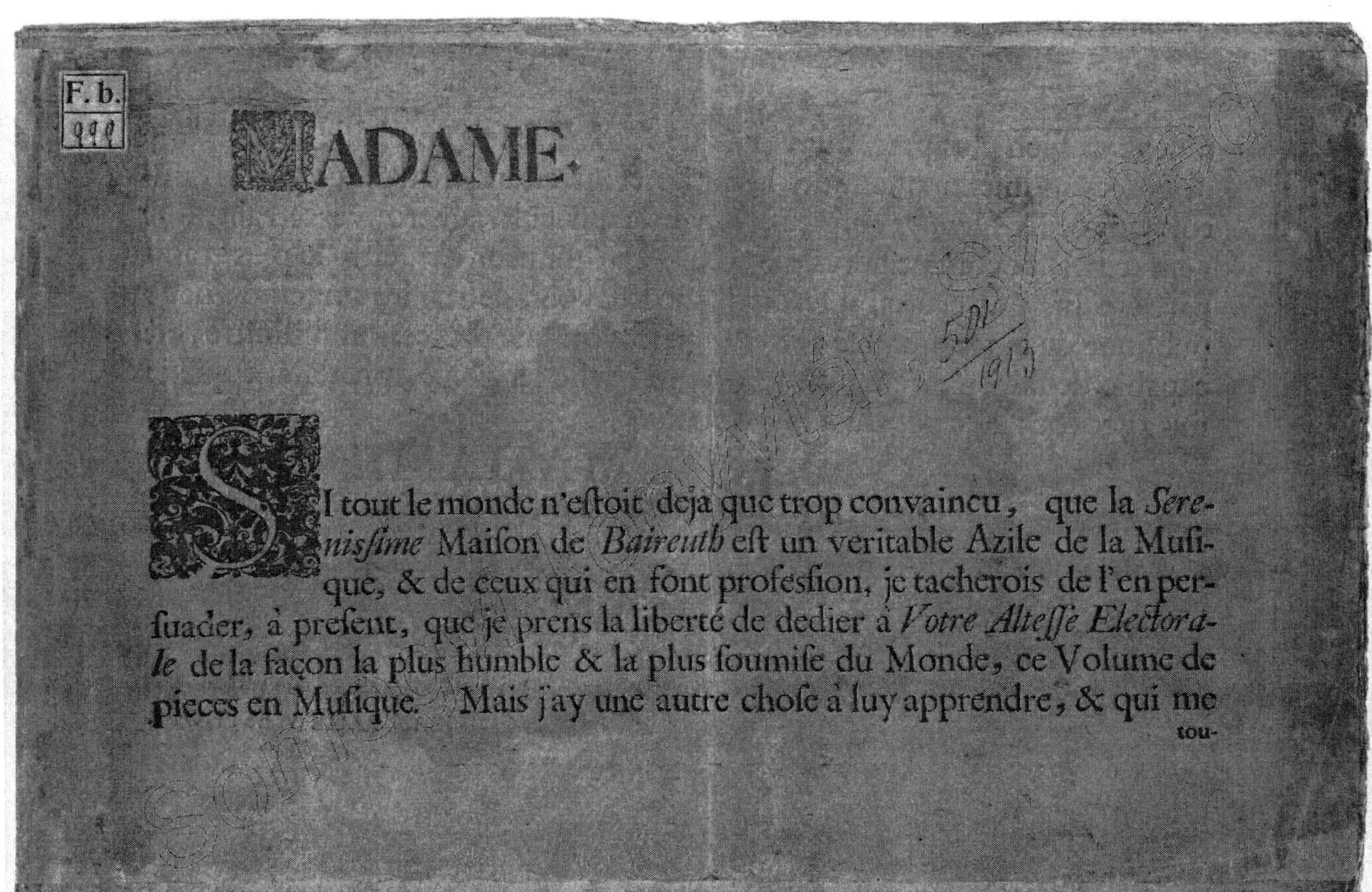

MADAME.

SI tout le monde n'eſtoit deja que trop convaincu, que la *Sereniſſime* Maiſon de *Baireuth* eſt un veritable Azile de la Muſique, & de ceux qui en font profeſsion, je tacherois de l'en perſuader, à preſent, que je prens la liberté de dedier à *Votre Alteſſe Electorale* de la façon la plus humble & la plus ſoumiſe du Monde, ce Volume de pieces en Muſique. Mais j'ay une autre choſe à luy apprendre, & qui me tou-

touche de bien plus prés, aſſavoir, que *V. A. E.* ſe fait un plaiſir de Combler de graces infinies une famille, la quelle etant etrangere dans ce pais ci, auroit ſans de ſi *Auguſtes* auſpices, bien de la difficulté, de trouver terrain pour s'enraciner, & comme aprés ma ſœur j'ay l'honneur d'en eſtre le plus grand participant, j'ay crû qu'il ſeroit de mon devoir, de rendre un temoignage publique de la tres humble reconnoiſſance qu'une protection ſi Illuſtre, eſt capable de faire naitre dans l'ame d'un fidelle ſerviteur, proteſtant que je ſuis avec tout le reſpet dû à ſa *Souveraine*

MADAME,

DE VOTRE ALTESSE ELECTORALE

à Dreſen le 6. Juil. 1696.

le tres humble tres ſoumis & tres acqvis ſujet

JEAN PAUL WESTHOFF.

Allemande

1.

adagio.

Allegro.

Ab

Courante

2.

Ab

3.

Sarabande

Ab

Gigue

4.

Ab

5.

Ab

Allomande

6.

Ah

7.

Ah

Courante 8.

Ah

9.

Sarabande.

Ah

Gigue.

10.

Ah

11

p. f.

Allemande 12.

B

Courante

13

Gigue

15.

f. P. f. B P.

16.

B

Allemande 17

p. f. C p. f.

Courante 18

C

Sarabande

19

p.

c

Gigue

20

p.

f.

c

21.

C

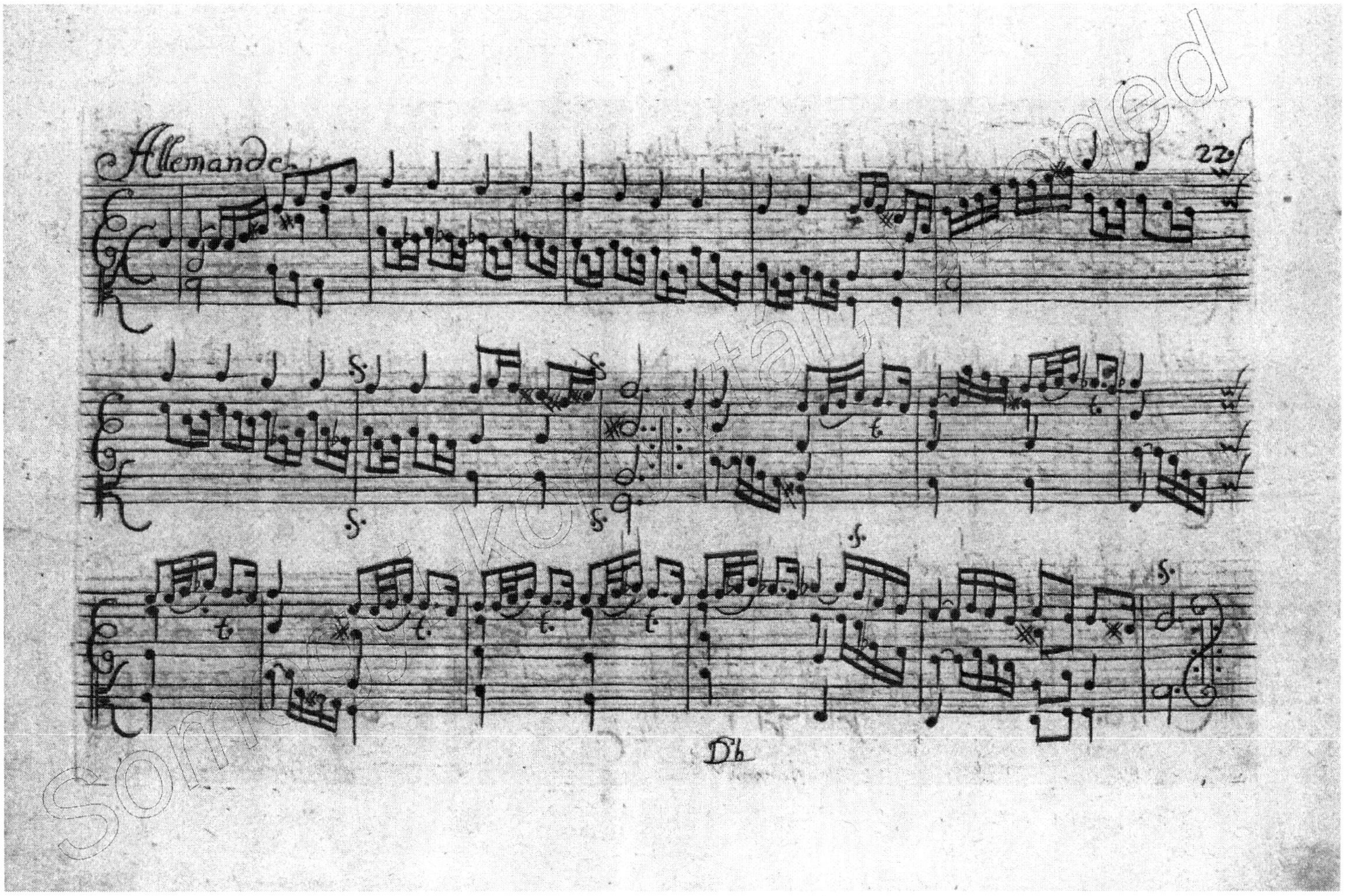

Allemande

22

Db

Coûrante

23

Db

Sarabante

24

Db

Gigue

25.

Db

36.

Db

Allemande 27.

D4

Courante 28.

D4

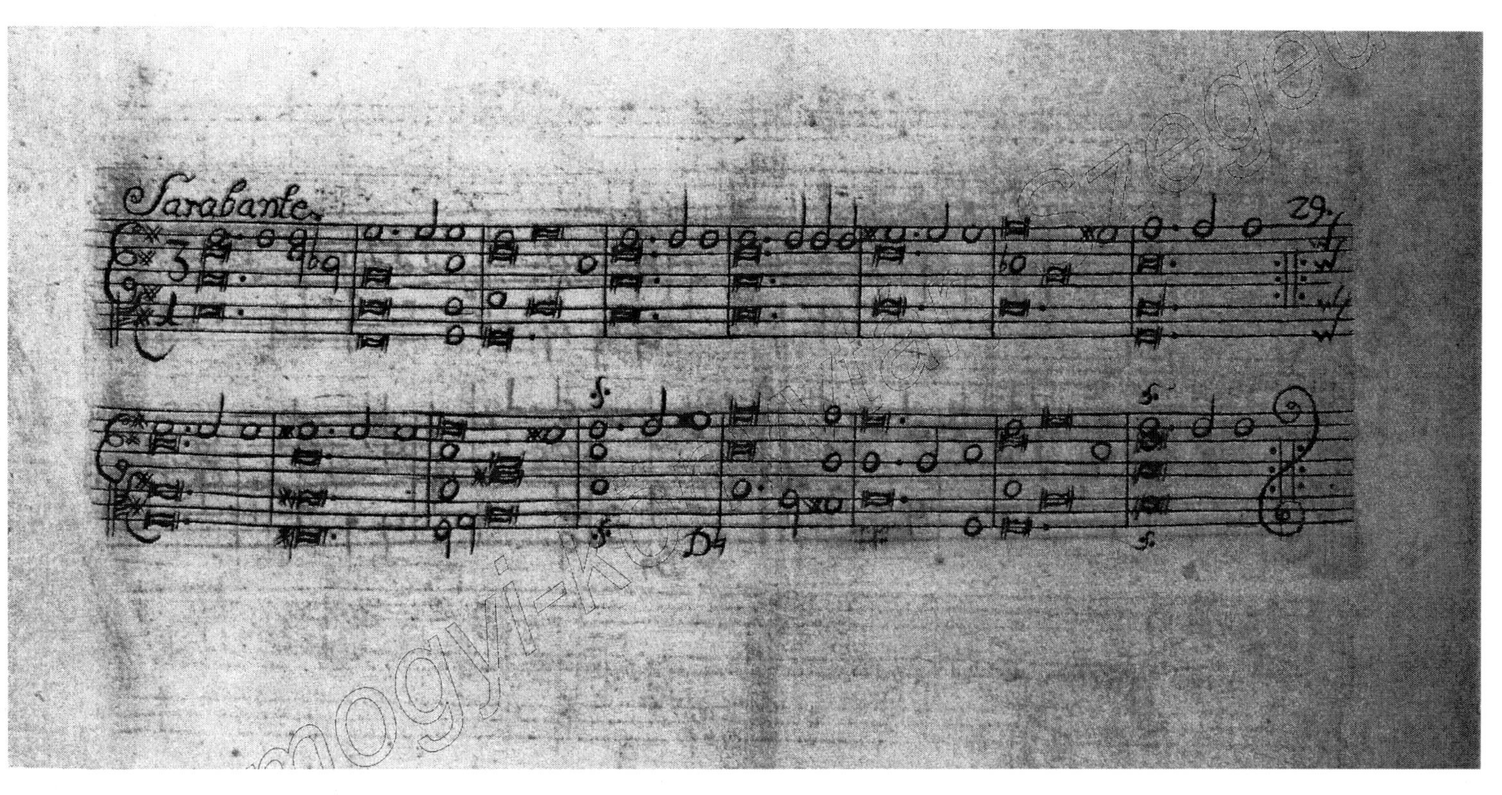

Gigve

30

D4

About the Author

Dr. Sarah Jones-Hayes *Photograph courtesy of Veronique Kherian*

Dr. Sarah Jones-Hayes has performed as soloist and chamber musician throughout the US, Europe and China. She has served on faculty at San Jose State University as Assistant Professor of Violin and Viola, Coordinator of Strings and Director of the SJSU String Project. She has held teaching positions at Arkansas State University (where she also served as Strings Area Coordinator, and director of the university orchestra and youth orchestra), Wayne State University and the University of Michigan. Dr. Jones has also taught at the Cleveland Institute of Music's preparatory department, Interlochen Summer Camp and Violin Institute and Interharmony International Music Festival in Acqui Terme, Italy. She has presented masterclasses at Southwest, Shenzen, Lingnan Normal and Shanqui Normal universities in China, The Music Academy in Olsztyn, Poland, Interlochen's Violin Institute, The University of Oregon, and The University of Oklahoma among others.

As an orchestral musician, Sarah has served as concertmaster of the North Mississippi Symphony Orchestra, and associate concertmaster of the Delta Symphony Orchestra. She has been a member of Canton Symphony Orchestra and has played with many of the San Francisco Bay Area orchestras as well as Dayton Philharmonic Orchestra, Springfield, Akron, Traverse, and Arkansas symphony orchestras. She has also appeared as soloist with the Polish Forum Sinfonia, Silicon Valley Philharmonic, Chamber Music Silicon Valley, Delta Symphony Orchestra, and the Southeastern Ohio Symphony Orchestra.

Dr. Jones holds a Doctor of Musical Arts in violin performance from the University of Michigan and received her Bachelor of Music in violin performance and Master of Music in violin performance and Suzuki pedagogy from the Cleveland Institute of Music. Her principal teachers include David Updegraff, Constantine Kiradjieff and David Halen.